WORLD WAR II

CAUSES OF WORLD WAR II

BY HEATHER C. HUDAK

CONTENT CONSULTANT
G. Kurt Piehler
Institute on World War II and the Human Experience
Florida State University

Cover image: Benito Mussolini, *left*, and Adolf Hitler, *right*, were extreme dictators. Their belief systems were a cause of World War II.

Core Library
An Imprint of Abdo Publishing
abdobooks.com

abdobooks.com

Published by Abdo Publishing, a division of ABDO, PO Box 398166, Minneapolis, Minnesota 55439.

Printed in the United States of America, North Mankato, Minnesota.
052024
092024

Cover Photo: Culture Club/Hulton Archive/Getty Images
Interior Photos: Keystone/Hulton Archive/Getty Images, 4–5; Heinrich Hoffmann/ullstein bild/Getty Images, 6, 17, 45; Hulton Deutsch/Corbis Historical/Getty Images, 8, 31; William Orpen/VCG Wilson/Fine Art/Corbis Historical/Getty Images, 12–13, 43; Red Line Editorial, 15, 38; Bettmann/Getty Images, 18–19, 20; Album/Alamy, 23; Herbert Hoffmann/ullstein bild/Getty Images, 26–27; Photo 12/Universal Images Group/Getty Images, 34–35; Historica Graphica Collection/Heritage Images/Hulton Archive/Getty Images, 36

Editor: Marley Richmond
Series Designer: Ryan Gale

Library of Congress Control Number: 2023949486

Publisher's Cataloging-in-Publication Data

Names: Hudak, Heather C., author.
Title: Causes of world war II / by Heather C. Hudak
Description: Minneapolis, Minnesota: Abdo Publishing, 2025 | Series: World war II | Includes online resources and index.
Identifiers: ISBN 9781098293642 (lib. bdg.) | ISBN 9798384912910 (ebook)
Subjects: LCSH: World War, 1939-1945--Juvenile literature. | War--Causes--Juvenile literature. | National socialism--Juvenile literature. | Germany--Juvenile literature. | Politics and government—Juvenile literature.
Classification: DDC 940.53--dc23

CONTENTS

UHREN P.

CHAPTER ONE

SETTING THE STAGE FOR CONFLICT

Thump. Thump. Thump. Thump. The sound of boots on the ground was unmistakable. German soldiers marched across the border into Austria on the morning of March 12, 1938. Ahead of them, a long line of trucks, tanks, and horses carried weapons and any other equipment the soldiers might need for battle. People rushed out of their homes to watch the fleet go by. Many people waved and cheered.

Many people waved flags to celebrate German troops entering Austria in March 1938.

German chancellor Adolf Hitler entered Austria at Braunau am Inn, where he was born. People saluted him when he arrived.

The Germans had come to annex Austria, and they faced no resistance. The annexation was part of the Anschluss, which would unify Germany and Austria. The two countries had a shared culture and ideals.

Many Austrians believed the Anschluss would improve their economy and rid their country of people whom they saw as unfavorable citizens.

German chancellor Adolf Hitler joined the march into Austria. It was his first visit to the country in more than 20 years. He was called a hero for making the Anschluss happen. Over the next three days, Hitler toured across Austria, greeting supporters along the way. The tour ended in Vienna, Austria. On March 15, Hitler spoke to a crowd of

PERSPECTIVES

ANTI-SEMITISM IN AUSTRIA

Adolf Hitler believed Jewish people were inferior and unfavorable citizens. He put anti-Semitic laws in place in Germany years before the Anschluss, and many Austrians wanted similar laws in their country. The Anschluss made this possible. It marked a time of terror for Jewish people in Austria. On March 11, 1938, many Jews tried to flee the country before it came under German control. But most didn't make it out. They were attacked, beaten, and robbed. Soon after, the same laws that discriminated against Jewish people in Germany were put in place in Austria.

Chancellor Kurt von Schuschnigg was openly against Hitler and his party. After Schuschnigg resigned, the Germans imprisoned him until World War II ended.

about 200,000 people. They cheered as Hitler declared that Austria would become part of Germany.

GERMAN-AUSTRIAN UNIFICATION

Most Austrians considered themselves to be ethnically German, and Hitler wanted to unite them all in one country. Many Austrians agreed. The country's economy was failing. People there thought their problems could be solved by becoming part of Germany. However, Austria had signed an agreement at the end of World War I (1914–1918) called the Treaty of Saint-Germain. It was between Austria and the Allied powers, which included France and Great Britain. The treaty prevented Austria and Germany from uniting. Allied leaders thought the countries would be too powerful together.

Hitler decided he wanted to unite the countries even if it meant breaking the Treaty of Saint-Germain. At first, he discussed his plan with Austrian chancellor Kurt von Schuschnigg. Schuschnigg wanted to let Austrians decide the issue. He scheduled a vote for March 13, 1938, but Hitler was too impatient. He pressured Schuschnigg into resigning on March 11.

VOTING ON THE ANSCHLUSS

An Austrian vote on the Anschluss took place on April 10, 1938, nearly a month after the annexation. Jewish people were not allowed to participate. Austrians who were allowed to cast a ballot voted more than 99 percent in favor. However, the ballots were not anonymous. Many people feared that if they voted against the annexation, they would be punished.

Immediately after Schuschnigg's resignation, Hitler's supporters in Austria began to take over government buildings. One day later, on March 12, Germany invaded. Austria became a German province called Ostmark.

THE WORLD AT WAR

World War I had ended in 1918. Over the next 20 years, many events contributed to the start of World War II (1939–1945). Several treaties were signed that were meant to prevent another global war. Peace organizations such as the League of Nations were created. This group was formed to peacefully resolve disputes between countries, but it often failed to do so.

The global economy also began to struggle. The rise of dictatorships in Germany and Japan led to conflict, as did Germany's continued expansion. These pressures built up until war broke out on September 1, 1939.

STRAIGHT TO THE SOURCE

Adolf Hitler gave a speech on April 9, 1938. It was the day before Austrians voted on whether they approved of the Anschluss. Hitler spoke about the German empire, or Reich. In German, he said:

> *When one day we shall be no more, then the coming generations shall be able to look back with pride upon this day, the day on which a great [people] affirmed the German community. In the past, millions of German men shed their blood for this Reich. How merciful a fate to be allowed to create this Reich today without a suffering.*
>
> *Now, rise, German [people], subscribe to it, hold it tightly in your hands! . . . May every German realize the importance of the hour tomorrow.*

Source: "Speech in Austria," April 9, 1938. *UNC Pembroke: Illuminating through Inquiry*. n.d., uncp.edu. Accessed 16 Oct. 2023.

WHAT'S THE BIG IDEA?

Take a close look at this passage. What point is Hitler making about the Anschluss? What can you tell about his values and beliefs according to this quote? Does it go beyond simply annexing Austria?

CHAPTER TWO

AFTER WORLD WAR I

The tensions that led to World War II began building immediately after World War I. The Allied powers imposed treaties on the defeated Central Powers, which included Germany. These treaties were meant to prevent another world war. One of the most notable was the Treaty of Versailles. None of the Central Powers were invited to take part in the discussions that led to the treaty.

The treaty declared that Germany was solely responsible for starting World War I. Germany was forced to give up much of the

In 1919, William Orpen painted *The Signing of Peace in the Hall of Mirrors*. The painting showed world leaders signing the Treaty of Versailles.

territory it controlled before the war. The country had to pay for all damages caused during World War I and was left with a massive debt. On top of that, the German military would be capped at 100,000 members, and Germany could not force people to join the military.

On June 28, 1919, Germany signed the Treaty of Versailles. Germans were not satisfied with the outcome. But the country's leaders felt they had no other choice.

LEAGUE OF NATIONS

The League of Nations was established as part of the Treaty of Versailles. If there was a threat to any member country, the other members of the league would support that country. Though US president Woodrow Wilson came up with the idea for the league, the United States was not a member. The US Senate voted against joining.

NAZI PARTY

Not long after the Treaty of Versailles went into effect, the National Socialist German Workers' Party, or Nazi Party, formed in Germany. It had extreme nationalist ideas about the future of Germany. The Nazis

EUROPE BEFORE AND AFTER WORLD WAR I

These maps show the national borders in Europe before and after World War I. The second map shows how countries' borders were changed by the Treaty of Versailles. How do these maps help you understand why Germans did not like this treaty?

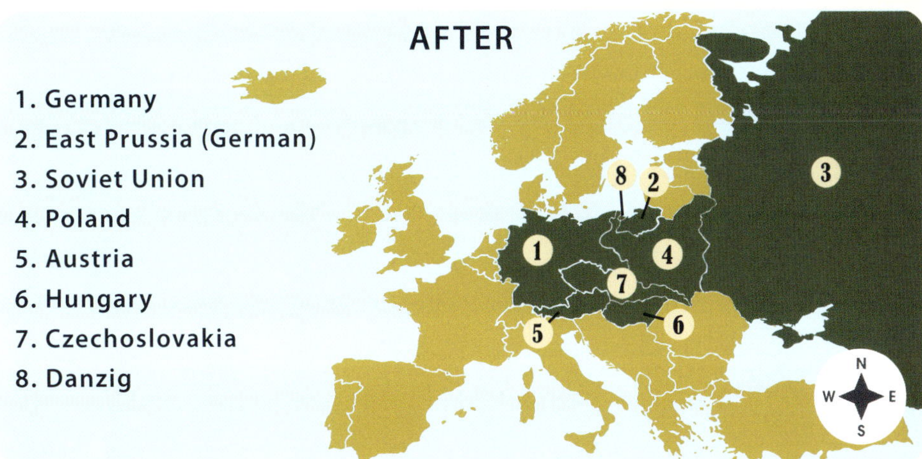

PERSPECTIVES

GERMAN CITIZENS UPSET

Many Germans were deeply upset about the Treaty of Versailles. They thought the punishments were too harsh. They did not think they should be blamed for the war. They were also angered by the loss of territory. A German newspaper in 1919 wrote, "The disgraceful Treaty is being signed today. Don't forget it! We will never stop until we win back what we deserve."

wanted to fight back against the Treaty of Versailles, and many people joined the party in agreement. A major goal for the Nazis was to expand the country and unite all ethnic Germans as part of a Greater Germany.

The Nazi Party was also racist. Nazis believed that people were from an inferior race if they did not have what Nazis considered to be pure German blood. In particular, the Nazis were anti-Semitic. They blamed Jewish people for losing World War I and harming the German economy.

Adolf Hitler played a key role in shaping the Nazi Party's beliefs. In a 1920 speech, Hitler said that one of

Hitler's supporters were heavily armed when they arrived in Munich, a city in Bavaria.

the party's final goals was to remove all Jewish people from Germany. By 1921 Hitler was the leader of the Nazi Party.

ATTEMPTED OVERTHROW

On November 8 and 9, 1923, Hitler and the Nazi Party tried to overthrow the government of Bavaria. They blamed this German state for its role in agreeing to the Treaty of Versailles. But their efforts failed.

Two days later, Hitler was arrested for betraying his country. He was sentenced to five years in prison, but he served less than nine months. Hitler decided he would only use legal methods to gain power.

CHAPTER THREE

EXTREME POLITICAL VIEWS

Following World War I, the huge costs of reparations left Germany with a weakened economy. Many people were unemployed and blamed the German government. People wanted change, and many saw the extreme politics of the Nazi Party as a path forward. Between 1925 and 1929, the Nazi Party grew from about 25,000 supporters to about 180,000. The party was still small, but it was growing.

The Nazi Party created many youth groups to teach children the beliefs and ideals of the Nazis. These groups helped the party continue to grow.

During the Great Depression, many people lost their life savings. Soup kitchens served meals to people who could not afford to buy food.

THE GREAT DEPRESSION

The German economy started to improve in 1924 with the help of loans from the United States. However, the loans stopped after the US economy took a severe downturn in October 1929. The crash was the start of the Great Depression. The depression started in the United States but quickly spread around the world.

Germany was forced to repay its debt early, and its banking system fell apart. Soon after, banks across Central Europe fell into crisis too. Unemployment rates rose and businesses closed. Countries began to limit trade with each other. This was a problem for countries such as Germany and Japan that did not have access to raw materials to produce their own goods.

THE SHŌWA DEPRESSION

Japan was also facing an economic crisis. After World War I, the country's economy had slowed down. By the late 1920s, a major financial institution in Japan went bankrupt. It caused panic across the country. The Great

PERSPECTIVES

US ISOLATIONISM

After World War I, the United States avoided entering any alliances or conflicts outside of North and South America. This policy was called isolationism. US leaders knew that many Americans would die if the country entered another war. The United States would not benefit enough to justify the casualties. US isolationism continued throughout the 1930s.

Depression made the situation worse, leading to the Shōwa Depression of 1930 to 1931. Many people were upset with the government for not doing more to help them. Much like the people of Germany, they wanted change.

As the economy grew weaker, some Japanese people started to develop extreme nationalist ideas. Japanese nationalists thought people from other cultures were inferior and wanted to rid Japan of outside influence. At the same time, many Japanese people believed the government was weak. They thought it could do more to protect Japanese interests.

THE MUKDEN INCIDENT

Many Japanese people admired the country's military for its strong sense of nationalism. The military wanted to showcase its power. Japan had troops stationed in the Manchuria region of China. In 1931 military officials in Manchuria plotted to invade Mukden, a Chinese city in the region. But they did not have approval

In September 1931, Japanese troops gathered outside Manchuria. They prepared for the invasion.

from the Japanese government. On September 18, the Japanese Army set off a bomb near a railroad. They blamed the Chinese Army for the incident and then occupied parts of China as a security measure.

The Japanese government did nothing to stop its own army as it took control over much of northeast China. Within months, Japanese forces had also taken control of large parts of Mongolia, and the army continued to advance across northern China. The League of Nations condemned the Mukden Incident, and Japan withdrew its membership from the organization.

FIRST CONCENTRATION CAMP

In 1933 Hitler put several anti-Jewish policies in place. He also founded the first concentration camp. It was in Dachau, Germany. The camp was a detention center for anyone who was seen as a political enemy of the state. Thousands of people were sent there in the first year alone. Throughout the 1930s, concentration camps were used to imprison people without a trial. Prisoners performed forced labor and faced extremely harsh living conditions. Many were tortured or killed.

GERMAN DICTATORSHIP

By 1932 the Nazi Party was the largest political party in Germany, but it still did not hold a majority of seats in parliament. Because of the Nazi Party's popularity, the president of Germany named Hitler chancellor on January 30, 1933. That made him the head of the German government. As planned, Hitler had risen to the top legally.

Hitler began to place restrictions on human rights and freedoms. He banned all political parties in Germany except the Nazi Party. He then began to take apart the democratic system of government and gave himself and the Nazi Party more power. In addition, he continued working to rid the world of Jewish people and anyone he saw as a threat.

FURTHER EVIDENCE

This chapter discusses the Great Depression. Visit the following website. Find a quote that supports the chapter's main point. Think about whether the quote supports an existing piece of evidence in the chapter or adds a new one.

GREAT DEPRESSION

abdocorelibrary.com/causes-world-war-ii

IA-85569
KRUPP

CHAPTER FOUR

EARLY ACTS OF AGGRESSION

In August 1934, the president of Germany died. Hitler declared himself führer, or leader, of Germany on August 19. Now he could do anything he wanted. Hitler had made Germany a dictatorship under his control.

When the Nazis took control of Germany, they quickly increased weapons production for their military. In 1935 Hitler reinstated mandatory military service in Germany. The military would increase in size to 500,000 members. These actions violated the Treaty of Versailles.

People paraded through the streets to celebrate Hitler becoming führer. Each flag showed a swastika, which was a symbol of the Nazi Party.

PERSPECTIVES

INVASION OF ETHIOPIA

Benito Mussolini was Italy's leader. He was a fascist dictator. Like Hitler, Mussolini wanted to expand the territory of his country. In October 1935, Italy invaded Ethiopia. Mussolini said, "The League of Nations . . . dares talk of sanctions, but until there is proof of the contrary, I refuse to believe that the authentic people of France will join in supporting sanctions against Italy." He was correct. Although the League of Nations condemned the invasion, not enough member countries supported attempts to punish Italy. The response showed that the League of Nations could not prevent conflict without powerful support.

RHINELAND TAKEOVER

The Rhineland was a part of Germany. It shared a border with France, Belgium, and the Netherlands. After World War I, a treaty stated that Germany could not have any military in this area.

In 1935 France signed a pact with the Soviet Union. Hitler saw this as a threat to Germany's security. He believed France would invade Germany through the Rhineland. On March 7, 1936,

Hitler ordered German troops to occupy the Rhineland despite the treaty.

The French government did not take any action against Germany after its invasion of the Rhineland. This was an example of appeasement. Appeasement is the act of giving a government what it wants in an attempt to prevent conflict. The French government hoped that by using appeasement, it could avoid a war. This failed and instead gave Hitler more power and control.

NUREMBERG LAWS

In September 1935, the Nazis announced anti-Jewish laws at a conference in Nuremberg, Germany. One law stated that Jewish people were no longer citizens of Germany. They did not have rights and could not vote.

Nazis believed that Jews were a threat to Germans. The Nuremberg Laws helped set the stage for future acts of violence against Jews. They were also meant to ensure that the next generation of Germans had what the Nazis considered to be pure German blood.

EXPANDING ALLIANCES

In November 1936, Japan and Germany signed the Anti-Comintern Pact. The pact said both countries would work together to oppose communism. Italy joined the pact in 1937. The pact implied that Germany, Japan, and Italy would work together against the Soviet Union, a Communist nation.

While Hitler was growing his territory in Europe, Japan continued expanding into China. Finally in 1937, China decided to push back against Japan. This marked

SPANISH CIVIL WAR

The Spanish Civil War (1936–1939) started in July 1936. It was fought between two groups called the Nationalists and Republicans. The Nationalists wanted to overthrow the democratically elected government, which the Republicans supported. Italy and Germany sent troops to help the Nationalists, who were supported by fascists. The Soviet Union sent supplies to aid the Republicans, who were supported by Communists. This war was an early example of the fight over ideologies that would play out in World War II.

German and Japanese representatives signed the Anti-Comintern Pact on November 25, 1936.

the beginning of the Second Sino-Japanese War, which would eventually become part of World War II.

MUNICH AGREEMENT

After the Anschluss in March 1938, Hitler set his sights on Sudetenland. Sudetenland was a part of Czechoslovakia with a large ethnically German population. Hitler wanted to reunite these Germans with their homeland. He threatened that he would go to war if Germany was not allowed to annex the area.

On September 30, 1938, Germany signed an agreement with France, Italy, and Great Britain called the Munich Agreement. In it, Germany was given control over Sudetenland. In exchange, Hitler promised to keep the peace. This agreement was another example of appeasement.

KRISTALLNACHT

On November 9 and 10, 1938, the sound of glass breaking could be heard across Germany, Austria, and Sudetenland. During Kristallnacht, or the Night of Broken Glass, the Nazis started a wave of violent acts against Jewish communities. Ninety-one Jews were killed during Kristallnacht, and 30,000 Jewish men were sent to concentration camps.

Hitler declared that Jewish people were to blame for the events. In the weeks that followed Kristallnacht, policies were put in place to prevent Jews from rebuilding their lives. Kristallnacht was a turning point for the Nazis, and their anti-Jewish actions increased.

STRAIGHT TO THE SOURCE

US president Franklin D. Roosevelt was outraged when he learned about Kristallnacht. He made a statement about it on November 15, 1938. He said:

> *The news of the past few days from Germany has deeply shocked public opinion in the United States. Such news from any part of the world would inevitably produce a similar profound reaction among American people in every part of the Nation. I myself could scarcely believe that such things could occur in a twentieth-century civilization.*

Source: "FDR Statement on Kristallnacht." *Jewish Virtual Library*, n.d., jewishvirtuallibrary.org. Accessed 20 Sept. 2023.

CONSIDER YOUR AUDIENCE

Review this passage closely. Consider how you would adapt it for a different audience, such as the people of Germany or European leaders. Write a speech conveying this same information to the new audience. What is the most effective way to get your point across to this audience? How does your new approach differ from the original text, and why?

CHAPTER FIVE

ON THE ROAD TO WAR

For years Hitler had worked to get the German people on his side. He had convinced them they needed extreme change. By 1939 Hitler was ready to take the next steps in his plan to expand Germany across Europe and rid the world of Jewish people.

REICHSTAG SPEECH

On January 30, 1939, Hitler addressed the German parliament, which was called the Reichstag. Hitler claimed it was necessary to

The Nazis used propaganda posters to spread their ideas. Many posters showed Hitler as a leader of the German people.

Members of the Reichstag saluted Hitler after his speech.

expand Germany in order to secure food and other resources for Germans. Hitler also made anti-Semitic claims that were untrue and meant to drive hatred toward Jews. For example, he said that Jewish people hurt the German economy and earned their money dishonestly. He said that if another world war were to break out, it would mean the end of Jews in Europe. Nazis planned to kill or imprison all European Jews.

Hitler told his people the only reason he needed to rearm the country was so it could protect itself in the event of an attack. In truth Hitler was planning to invade other countries. He was preparing the nation for battle.

PREPARING FOR WAR

On March 15, 1939, Germany broke the Munich Agreement and invaded Czechoslovakia. Tensions rose across Europe. On August 23, 1939, the Nazis signed the German-Soviet Nonaggression Pact. It said that Germany and the Soviet Union would not attack each other for at least ten years. As part of the pact, each country secretly claimed parts of Eastern Europe that they planned to invade.

Germany was growing stronger, which caused concerns about a possible war in Europe. Poland feared it would be attacked over the Polish Corridor. This strip of land had once belonged to Germany, but it was given to Poland in the Treaty of Versailles. On August 25, Poland and Great Britain signed the Anglo-Polish Pact of Mutual Assistance. It stated that Great Britain would come to Poland's aid in the event of a German invasion. France also said it would provide support.

On September 1, 1939, German troops invaded Poland. This would become the official start of World

THE POLISH CORRIDOR

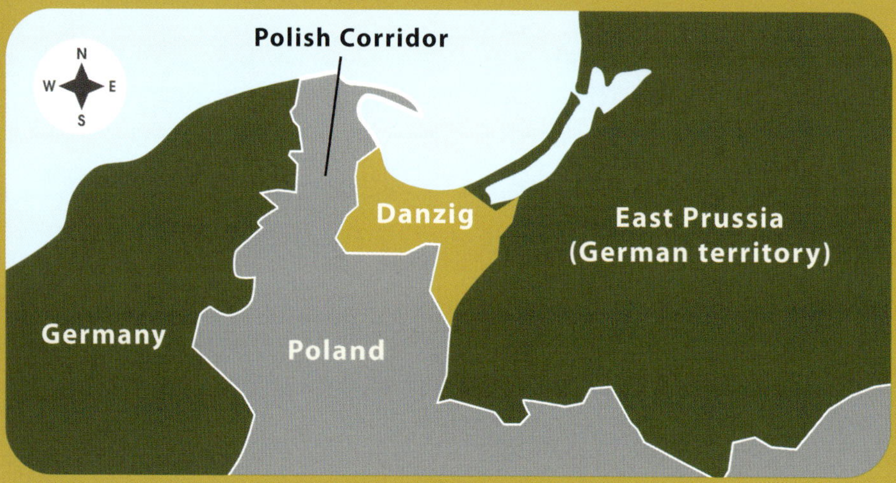

This map shows the Polish Corridor, which split Germany's territory in two. Danzig was a free city overseen by the League of Nations following the Treaty of Versailles. How does this map help you understand Germany's decision to invade Poland?

War II. Great Britain declared war on Germany on September 3, and France followed suit the same day. Soon countries across Europe and around the world became engaged in battle.

CONFLICT IN THE PACIFIC

As World War II began to rage in Europe, the Second Sino-Japanese War was still going on between China and Japan. Based on its policy of isolationism, the

United States avoided getting involved in either conflict throughout the 1930s. However, by 1940, US president Franklin D. Roosevelt became concerned with the growing size and power of the Empire of Japan. Roosevelt sent aid to China to support that country's war effort and began restricting exports to Japan.

In September 1940, Japan signed a pact with Germany and Italy. This connected the conflicts in Europe and Asia. Japan turned its military attention to Southeast Asia. The United States saw Japan's actions as a threat. President Roosevelt placed an embargo on Japan. The United States stopped much-needed exports from being sent to Japan.

TRIPARTITE PACT

On September 27, 1940, Germany, Italy, and Japan signed the Tripartite Pact. Together, they were known as the Axis powers. The three countries agreed to defend each other if any of them came under attack by a country that was not already part of the war in Europe or the Second Sino-Japanese War in Asia. The pact was called into action when the United States declared war on Japan in 1941.

US leaders hoped this would force Japan to stop its aggressive actions.

PERSPECTIVES

US REACTION TO WORLD WAR II

When the Allied powers in Europe declared war on Germany, President Roosevelt said the United States would not join the war effort. At first, Americans were divided over the issue. In May of 1940, 93 percent of Americans still supported the United States' decision to stay out of the war. As time went on, their opinions changed. Days after the Japanese attack on Pearl Harbor, more than 90 percent of Americans agreed with the United States' decision to declare war on Germany and Japan.

JAPAN RETALIATES

In the fall of 1941, Japan and the United States tried to negotiate a resolution of their differences in Asia. But Japan refused to stop its expansion in Asia and the Pacific. On December 7, 1941, Japan made its next move. Japanese planes dropped bombs on the US naval base at Pearl Harbor in Hawaii.

Japanese leaders wanted to distract the US military while Japanese forces invaded territories in the Pacific. The next day, the United States declared war on Japan. In response, Germany and Italy declared war on the United States. The United States had officially entered World War II.

Throughout World War II, Germany continued expanding through Europe. Japan fought to grow its empire in the Pacific. The Allied powers fought back against the Axis powers' expansion and their extreme governments. Many lives would be lost before World War II came to an end in 1945.

EXPLORE ONLINE

This chapter talks about the United States' embargo on Japan. Explore the following website and compare and contrast the information presented in this chapter with information on the website.

WHY DID JAPAN ATTACK PEARL HARBOR?

abdocorelibrary.com/causes-world-war-ii

IMPORTANT DATES

June 28, 1919
Germany signs the Treaty of Versailles.

October 1929
The Great Depression starts in the United States.

September 18, 1931
Japan invades Manchuria, China, as a display of military power.

August 19, 1934
Adolf Hitler declares himself the führer of Germany.

September 30, 1938
Germany signs the Munich Agreement with France, Italy, and Great Britain.

September 1, 1939
Germany invades Poland. World War II officially begins.

December 7, 1941
Japan bombs the US naval base at Pearl Harbor.

December 8, 1941
The United States declares war on Japan and enters World War II.

STOP AND THINK

Take a Stand

The United States had a policy of isolationism throughout the 1930s. President Roosevelt condemned the actions of both Germany and Japan, but he took no official action against them until the 1940s. Do you think this was the right approach to take? Or do you think the United States should have become involved earlier? Why?

Tell the Tale

Chapter One of this book discusses the Anschluss. Imagine you are a person of German descent living in Austria. Write 200 words about how you might have felt when German troops arrived. Would you have welcomed them into the country or not?

Surprise Me

Chapter Three discusses the Mukden Incident. After reading this book, what two or three facts about this event did you find most surprising? Write a few sentences about each fact. Why did you find each fact surprising?

Another View

This book talks about Adolf Hitler and his rise to power as the dictator of Germany. As you know, every source is different. Ask a librarian or another adult to help you find another source about Hitler. Write a short essay comparing and contrasting the new source's point of view with that of this book's author. What is the point of view of each author? How are they similar and why? How are they different and why?

GLOSSARY

annex
to take over one country's land and add it to another country

communism
a system of government that values common ownership over private property

dictatorship
the total control of one leader over a country or government

embargo
a ban on trading with another country

ethnically
having to do with racial, national, or cultural backgrounds

fascist
relating to a person who believes that the good of a nation is more important than that of individuals

nationalist
relating to the belief that one nation is better than others and that other nations should be more like it

reparations
payment made to repair something or make amends for having done something wrong

treaty
an official agreement between countries

ONLINE RESOURCES

To learn more about the causes of World War II, visit our free resource websites below.

Visit **abdocorelibrary.com** or scan this QR code for free Common Core resources for teachers and students, including vetted activities, multimedia, and booklinks, for deeper subject comprehension.

Visit **abdobooklinks.com** or scan this QR code for free additional online weblinks for further learning. These links are routinely monitored and updated to provide the most current information available.

LEARN MORE

Adams, Simon. *World War II*. DK, 2021.

Halls, Kelly Milner. *World War II History for Kids.* Rockridge, 2021.

Lim, Angela. *World War II in the Pacific*. Abdo, 2025.

INDEX

About the Author

Heather C. Hudak has written hundreds of children's books. When she's not writing, she enjoys traveling. She has been to nearly 60 countries and has visited World War I and World War II memorials all over the world. Heather's maternal grandmother and grandfather were both veterans of World War II. The events of that war have had a vast impact on her family's history.